Sleepy Littl Caterpillar

by Anne Giulieri
illustrated by Mélanie Florian

Look!

Here comes Little Caterpillar.

Little Caterpillar is sleepy.

Little Caterpillar looks at the pot.

"This pot is too big," said Little Caterpillar.

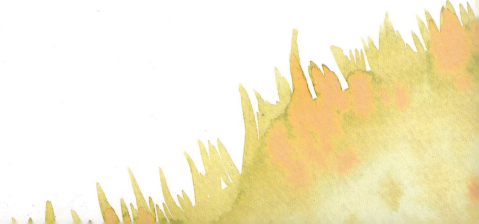

Little Caterpillar looks at the log.

"This log is too big,"
said Little Caterpillar.

Little Caterpillar looks at the leaf.

"This leaf is little," said Little Caterpillar. "I can go up the leaf."

Up, up, up!

Little Caterpillar is on the leaf.

Little Caterpillar is sleepy.

Here comes Little Butterfly.